you're the chef

a cookbook companion for *a smart girl's guide: cooking*

by Lisa Cherkasky

photography by Chris Hynes

illustrations by Elisa Chavarri

Published by American Girl Publishing

16 17 18 19 20 21 22 LEO 10 9 8 7 6 5 4 3 2 1

Editorial Development: Trula Magruder, Darcie Johnston
Art Direction and Design: Gretchen Becker
Photography: Chris Hynes Studio, Derek Brabender
Food Styling: Lisa Cherkasky, Carolyn Robb Schimley, Stef Culberson (cover)
Production: Jeannette Bailey, Cynthia Stiles, Kristi Tabrizi, Laura Markowitz
Illustrations: Elisa Chavarri
Consultant: Kevin Appleton

Library of Congress Cataloging-in-Publication Data
Cherkasky, Lisa, 1956- author.
You're the chef : a cookbook companion for a smart girl's guide : cooking /
by Lisa Cherkasky ; illustrated by Elisa Chavarri. — First edition.
pages   cm. — (A smart girl's guide)
Audience: Ages 10+.
ISBN 978-1-60958-737-6 (pbk.) — ISBN 978-1-60958-807-6 (ebook)
1. Cooking—Juvenile literature. I. Chavarri, Elisa, illustrator. II. Title.
TX652.5.C455 2016   641.5'123—dc23   2015020860

Safety Note
Even though instructions have been tested and results from testing were incorporated into this book, all recommendations and suggestions are made without any guarantees on the part of American Girl. Because of differing tools, materials, ingredients, conditions, and individual skills, the publisher disclaims liability for any injuries, losses, or other damages that may result from using the information in this book. Knives, ovens and stoves, hot dishes and ingredients, uncooked food, and powered appliances can cause severe injury. *Adult supervision is required at all times when following any instruction in this book.*

americangirl.com/service

Dear Reader,

Why cook when you can find a restaurant on every corner? Because cooking is one of life's greatest pleasures!

It's all about making people happy and nurturing them while you do it. And it's easier than you think. You don't have to get fancy to be a fantastic cook. All you need to do is learn some basic cooking techniques, figure out how to read a recipe, and get to know your kitchen equipment. It's really that simple.

This book gives you enough different recipes to teach you many of these skills. You'll learn how to make the dishes that every cook should know—and also how to create fun party food and unique snacks that everyone will love. Best of all, mastering these recipes will help you take charge of the kitchen and your table.

So if you love the idea of eating delicious food, feeding your family and friends, and having fun in the heart of your home, this book is for you. You *are* the chef!

Your friends at American Girl

safety first

Know these rules by heart before you start so that cooking will always be a fun experience for you.

Dress smart. Keep your hair back, wear closed-toe shoes, and avoid jewelry or clothing that dangles or drapes, such as hoodie strings or billowy sleeves.

Reach right. Use a sturdy step stool to reach high places in the kitchen. One with a handle on the back is best.

Hot stuff. Stay in the kitchen when food is cooking on the stove. Keep pot handles turned away from the edge of your stove, but make sure they aren't positioned over a hot burner either. Never put your face close to a pot when removing its lid—the hot steam can burn you. And if a pot is heavy or large, or if it contains boiling liquid, don't handle it yourself. Ask an adult to do it.

Wash up. Before, during, and after cooking, wash your hands often with soap and warm water, especially when handling meat. Wash counters with a soapy sponge, too. And wash all fruits and veggies in plenty of cold tap water, even if you're peeling the skin off.

React right. If a knife, skillet, or pot starts to fall, let it go—and quickly get out of the way. If you cut or burn yourself, let the adult helping you know right away. And if a fire starts, yell! Never try to put it out yourself.

FIRST RULE OF SAFETY

Almost every recipe in this book involves heat, knives and other sharp tools, powered appliances, or raw foods (which may have germs). **ADULT SUPERVISION IS REQUIRED AT ALL TIMES.**

recipe tips

A recipe tells you what ingredients and tools you need. It tells you how to make the dish, step by step. It's the voice of the original cook talking directly to you!

Read the entire recipe before you start cooking. This will tell you in advance what you'll need to shop for, what kitchen tools to have on hand, how long it will take to make the dish, and even any cooking terms you might need to look up.

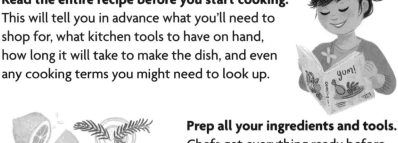

Prep all your ingredients and tools. Chefs get everything ready before they start cooking. You'll want to do this, too. First, read the recipe carefully. Then set out each ingredient and tool you'll be using. Also, wash and chop fruits and vegetables, measure out the ingredients, and place everything in separate bowls.

Measure carefully! When measuring, you need the right tool. For liquids, use a clear spouted cup with measurements printed down the side. Place it on the counter, add the liquid, and bend down until your eye is level with the mark you want. Is the liquid exactly at the right mark? If not, add more

or pour some out. For dry ingredients, use a scooping cup or spoon. Fill the cup or spoon until it's overflowing—and don't pack it in tight unless the recipe says to do so. Then use the flat edge of a butter knife to scrape across the top, removing the excess.

Follow your instincts. Recipes turn out best when you give them your personal attention. Does the dish taste like it needs a little salt? Another squeeze of lemon? A longer cooking time? The more you cook, the more your instincts and experience will guide you.

cooking terms & tools

Recipes might call for a technique or tool that's new to you. If so, ask a parent what it is or look it up. Here are some of the most common.

Slice: to cut across and straight down, making equally thick or thin sections

Chop: to cut into pieces about ½-inch square

Mince: to cut into tiny pieces

Dice: to cut into small cubes

Pack: to press a food firmly into a cup with the back of a spoon when measuring

Pinch: ⅛ teaspoon

Sauté: to cook food in oil or butter on the stove top at medium heat, stirring often

Boil: to cook a liquid on the stove top at high heat so that large bubbles form on the surface; when the bubbles are very large and active, it's called a *rolling* or *rapid* boil

Simmer: to cook a liquid on the stove top at a low heat so that only tiny bubbles ripple across the liquid's surface

Fry: like sautéing, except frying usually involves larger pieces of food, such as meat, that are turned once or twice instead of stirred

Bake: to cook food such as cakes and casseroles in an uncovered pan in the oven; baking usually browns the surface of the food

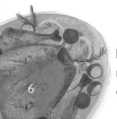

Roast: like baking, except roasting refers to meats or vegetables

Whisk: to mix ingredients very quickly with a whisk—a special tool made of loops—until the mixture is thick and creamy or light and frothy

Stir: to mix ingredients together with a slow, circular motion

Beat: to mix ingredients with a fast motion, using either an electric mixer or a cooking spoon

Skillet: a shallow pan used to cook or fry food on the stove top; many have lids

Roasting pan: a wide metal pan used for roasting large pieces of meat in the oven; some come with a rack or a lid

Saucepan: a deeper pan used to cook food on the stove top; they come in many sizes and usually have lids

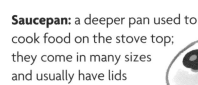

Baking dish: a ceramic or glass pan used for baking all kinds of foods in the oven; they come in different sizes and may have lids

Baking sheet: a flat metal pan with shallow or no sides, used for baking many kinds of foods, such as cookies or pizza, in the oven

Nonstick pan: a pan made with a coating that helps keep food from sticking to it

planning a meal

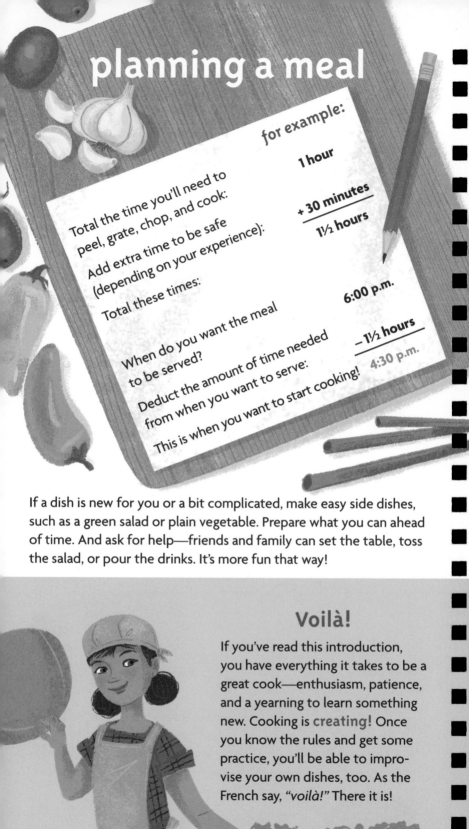

Total the time you'll need to peel, grate, chop, and cook:

Add extra time to be safe (depending on your experience):

Total these times:

When do you want the meal to be served?

Deduct the amount of time needed from when you want to serve:

This is when you want to start cooking!

for example:

1 hour

+ 30 minutes

1½ hours

6:00 p.m.

– 1½ hours

4:30 p.m.

If a dish is new for you or a bit complicated, make easy side dishes, such as a green salad or plain vegetable. Prepare what you can ahead of time. And ask for help—friends and family can set the table, toss the salad, or pour the drinks. It's more fun that way!

Voilà!

If you've read this introduction, you have everything it takes to be a great cook—enthusiasm, patience, and a yearning to learn something new. Cooking is **creating!** Once you know the rules and get some practice, you'll be able to improvise your own dishes, too. As the French say, *"voilà!"* There it is!

breakfast
& brunch

bitty berry pancakes
10

summer frittata
12

homemade granola
14

fruit salad with honey yogurt
16

fruity smoothie
18

bitty berry pancakes

These sweet pancakes aren't just for breakfast! Try them for dinner, slumber parties, and Mother's or Father's Day. For variety, replace the blueberries with equal amounts of other fruits or chocolate chips.

Makes about twenty 3-inch pancakes

Unsalted butter 4 tablespoons

All-purpose flour 1 cup

Granulated sugar 1 tablespoon

Baking soda 1 teaspoon

Salt ½ teaspoon

Egg 1 large

Buttermilk 1¼ cups

Vegetable-oil spray

Blueberries 2 cups

Toppings such as fruit, syrup, butter, jam, applesauce, yogurt, or powdered sugar

 Ask an adult to help with the stove.

1. **Prep the ingredients.** Wash and drain the berries; set them aside. Melt the butter in a small saucepan on the stove, using low heat.

2. **Mix the ingredients.** In a medium-size bowl, use a whisk to mix together the flour, sugar, baking soda, and salt. In a separate, large bowl, crack and thoroughly whisk the egg; then whisk in the buttermilk and melted butter. Pour the dry ingredients into the wet ingredients in the large bowl, and whisk together until just mixed. It's fine to have some small lumps.

3. **Pour batter onto the pan.** Coat a skillet or griddle with vegetable-oil spray, set it on the stove, and turn the burner to medium heat. When the pan is hot, dip into the batter with a ¼-cup measuring cup and pour it onto the pan. Space the pancakes so they don't touch—try only one or two at first.

4. **Add the berries.** Immediately drop 6 blueberries (or a different addition) onto each pancake, and lightly press them into the batter with the spatula tip. When bubbles have formed in the pancake, test it with the spatula to see if it's firm enough to flip.

5. **Flip the pancakes.** When ready, flip the pancake over and let it cook 1 minute on the second side. Slip the spatula tip into the center of the pancake. If it comes out clean, it's done. Cook the remaining batter, following steps 3–5.

6. **Finish with the toppings.** Serve the pancakes hot with an assortment of favorite toppings.

summer frittata

A frittata makes any meal seem special. If serving one for breakfast or brunch, add a side of fresh fruit and buttered toast. For lunch or dinner, all you need is a chunk of good bread and a crisp salad.

Makes 4 to 6 servings

Onion 1 medium

Red bell pepper 1 medium

Zucchini or yellow squash 1 medium

Spinach fresh, 3 cups

Cheese such as cheddar, Jack, or mozzarella; grated, ¾ cup

Parmesan cheese grated, ¾ cup

Extra-virgin olive oil 3 tablespoons

Eggs 10 large

Salt ½ teaspoon

Ground black pepper ¼ teaspoon

 Ask an adult to help with the knives, grater, stove, and oven.

---

1. **Prep the ingredients.** Wash all the vegetables. Peel and chop the onion and bell pepper, and thinly slice the zucchini or squash. Measure the spinach. Grate the cheeses.

2. **Cook the veggies.** Pour the oil into a large *ovenproof* skillet, turn the burner on to medium, and heat the pan for 2 minutes. Stir the onion, bell pepper, and zucchini or squash into the oil and cook for 5 to 7 minutes, until they are soft. Stir often.

3. **Add the spinach.** Add the spinach to the vegetables, turn the heat to low, and stir until the spinach wilts, about 1 minute. Turn the burner off for now, and leave the skillet there.

4. **Turn on the broiler.** Put the oven rack in an upper but not top position. Turn the oven on to the "broil" setting, so that it can start heating up.

5. **Whisk the eggs.** Break the eggs into a large mixing bowl. Add the cheeses, salt, and pepper. Whisk well.

6. **Cook the eggs.** Turn the burner back on to medium. Pour the egg mixture into the skillet with the veggies, and cook for 7 minutes—but don't stir! When the frittata is firm around the edges and still a bit liquid in the middle, slide the skillet into the oven. Check often! As soon as the frittata browns on top, remove it.

7. **Sit and serve.** Let the frittata rest for a minute, and then cut it into wedges. Serve it right out of the skillet, or use a pie server or spatula to lift the wedges onto a platter.

homemade granola

For a delicious breakfast, serve granola with fresh fruit and milk. For a healthy snack, sprinkle it on yogurt. And for dessert, spoon it over vanilla ice cream. What can *you* do with granola?

Makes 6 cups

Old-fashioned rolled oats (not quick-cooking or instant) 3 cups

Sunflower seeds ½ cup

Pecan or walnut pieces ¾ cup

Almonds ¾ cup

Salt ½ teaspoon

Vegetable oil 2 tablespoons

Honey or maple syrup ¼ cup

Brown sugar packed, 2 tablespoons

Dried cranberries and/or other dried fruit, 1 cup total

Ask an adult to help with the oven and stirring hot food.

1. **Turn on the oven.** Preheat to 325 degrees.

2. **Mix the dry ingredients.** In a large mixing bowl, combine the uncooked oats, seeds, nuts, and salt.

3. **Add the oil and sweeteners.** In a small bowl, stir together the oil, honey or syrup, and brown sugar. Pour this over the oat mixture and stir well, making sure to evenly coat all the ingredients.

4. **Bake, stir, bake, stir, bake, and stir.** Spread the granola out in an even layer on a large baking sheet with sides. Set the timer for 15 minutes, and place the pan in the oven. When the timer sounds, remove the pan from the oven, place it on the stove, and stir the granola. Bake for 10 minutes more, remove the pan, and stir again. Bake 10 minutes more, for a total bake time of 35 minutes. Remove the granola a final time, and stir in the dried fruit.

5. **Cool and store.** Let the granola cool completely. Then spoon it into an airtight container or a zip-seal bag, and store it in the refrigerator.

fruit salad with honey yogurt

Almost any combo of fruits is yummy with honey yogurt dressing. Berries? Any kind. Mango? Add chunks of that. Pears, peaches, or plums? Core, chop, and go for it!

Makes 4 to 6 servings

Strawberries ¾ cup

Seedless grapes 1½ cups

Kiwi 1 medium

Raspberries ¾ cup

Blueberries 1 cup

Orange 1 medium

Banana 1 medium

Plain yogurt 1 cup

Honey 2 tablespoons

 Ask an adult to help with the knives, peeler, and zester.

1. **Prep the fruit.** Wash the fruits, and remove any leaves or stems. Slice the strawberries and grapes. Peel and slice the kiwi. Put the cut fruit into a large bowl. Add the raspberries and blueberries, and gently mix the fruit together.

2. **Make the zest and juice.** Use a zester to grate the peel off the orange. (Or remove the zest with a peeler, and slice it into thin strips.) Set the zest aside. Cut the orange in half crosswise, and squeeze the juice over the fruit in the bowl.

3. **Add the banana.** Peel and slice the banana, and gently stir it into the salad. Bananas turn brown fast, so add them at the last minute.

4. **Make the dressing.** Whisk together the yogurt, honey, and most of the zest in a small bowl. Spoon the fruit into serving bowls, and add a dollop of the dressing to each one. Garnish with the zest.

17

fruity smoothie

Swirl up a sweet drink for breakfast or a snack. Try fresh or frozen berries, peaches, pineapples, or mangoes.

Makes 2 servings

Fresh or frozen fruit 1 cup

Banana 1 medium

Quick-cooking oatmeal (not instant or old-fashioned) 4 tablespoons

Fruit juice ½ cup

Vanilla yogurt 4 tablespoons

Ice if using fresh fruit, 4 cubes

 Ask an adult to help with the blender.

1. **Prep the fruit.** If using fresh fruit, wash it and chop it into chunks. Peel the banana, and break it into pieces.

2. **Prep the oatmeal.** Put the uncooked oatmeal in a blender, cover it with the juice, and whirl the blender for 10 seconds. Then let it soak for 1 minute.

3. **Blend and serve.** Add the yogurt, banana, fruit, and ice cubes (if using them) to the blender. Put the lid on tight. Whirl on high speed until smooth. Pour into a tall glass and drink up!

soups & sandwiches

turkey BLT
20

hummus pita pouch
21

chicken, egg, or tuna salad
22

gooey grills
24

chilly-day chili
26

Italian minestrone
28

quick chick soup
30

turkey BLT

A mouthwatering BLT relies on great tomatoes, so make your sandwich when tomatoes are bursting with flavor.

Makes 1 sandwich

Tomato 2 slices

Lettuce 1 leaf

Mayonnaise 1 tablespoon

Bread 2 slices

Sliced cooked turkey 2 pieces

Cooked bacon 3 slices

 Ask an adult to help with the knives and pre-cooking.

1. **Prep the vegetables and bread.** Wash and slice the tomato. Wash a lettuce leaf, and let it dry. Spread half the mayonnaise evenly over each slice of bread.

2. **Layer the ingredients.** Add the sandwich fillings to one slice of bread, and top with the second slice. For variety, try a turkey BLAT by adding sliced avocado.

hummus pita pouch

Hummus comes in many flavors, so try this sandwich again and again. Plus, these pouches travel well to school, practices, or picnics.

Makes 1 sandwich

Tomato 2 slices	**Carrot** shredded, ¼ cup
Cucumber 4 slices	**Pita bread** half of a 6-inch round
Avocado 3 slices	**Prepared hummus** ¼ cup

 Ask an adult to help with the knives, grater, and microwave.

1. **Prep the veggies.** Wash the veggies. Slice the tomato, and peel and slice the cucumber. Run a paring knife around the avocado, twist it open, remove the large seed (called the pit), peel off the skin, and cut it into slices. Use a grater to shred the carrot.

2. **Fill the bread.** Warm the pita in a toaster, or microwave it for 20 seconds—it should open up and form a pocket for filling. Spread the hummus inside the pita, and add the veggies.

chicken, egg, or tuna salad

Which came first, the chicken or the egg—or maybe the fish? When it comes to lunch, you get to choose!

Cooked chicken ⅓ cup OR
Hard-boiled eggs 2 large OR
Canned tuna ⅓ cup

Onion minced, 1 tablespoon

Celery minced, 1 tablespoon

Mayonnaise 1½ tablespoons

Salt ¼ teaspoon

Ground black pepper pinch

Bread, toast, lettuce, or crackers for serving

 Ask an adult to help with knives, boiling water, and pre-cooking.

1. **Prep the protein.** If using chicken, dice it. If using eggs, peel and chop them. If using tuna, drain it. Place the chicken, eggs, or tuna in a bowl. Use a fork to squish the eggs or break up the tuna.

2. **Prep the veggies.** Wash the onion, cut off a slice, and mince it. Wash and mince a small piece of celery. Add a tablespoon of each to the protein.

3. **Finish and serve.** Add the mayo, salt, and pepper, and stir to combine. Spoon the filling between slices of bread or toast, wrap it in a lettuce leaf, or scoop it onto crackers.

Hard-Boiled Eggs

Gently lay eggs in a saucepan, and add cold water to a level 1 or 2 inches above the eggs. Put the pan on the stove, turn the burner to medium-high, and heat until the water starts to boil. Turn off the heat, cover the pan with a lid, and set a timer for 15 minutes. After the timer goes off, move the eggs from the pan to a bowl of cold water. Once the eggs are cooled, peel them, rinsing until all the shell is gone, or store in the fridge.

gooey grills

Serve a bowl of soup with grilled cheese or
a fruit salad with grilled PBJ & B for a complete meal.

Bread 2 slices

Butter 2 teaspoons

For grilled cheese:

Cheddar or other cheese,
2 slices

For PBJ & B:

Peanut butter 1½ tablespoons

Jelly or jam 1½ tablespoons

Banana sliced, ½ medium

 Ask an adult to help with the stove.

1. **Make a sandwich.** Place the bread on a clean surface. Butter one side of each slice. On the unbuttered side of one slice, layer on the cheese or the peanut butter, jelly, and banana slices. Place the other bread slice on top, with the buttered side facing out.

2. **Cook until golden brown.** Place a skillet on the stove, and turn the burner to medium-low. Cook the sandwich until the bread is golden brown on the bottom. Lift a corner with a spatula to take a peek. After the bottom is toasted, slide the spatula under the sandwich and turn it over carefully. Cook until the second side is golden brown and the center is melted. Use the spatula to lift the sandwich out of the pan.

Waffle Sandwich!

For a yummy option, grill the sandwich in a waffle iron. After preheating the iron, place the buttered sandwich on the iron and close the lid. Check it often! When it's golden brown, take it out with tongs or a fork.

chilly-day chili

Cooking for a crowd? Chili is the perfect choice. Make it a day ahead, and it'll taste even better. Serve chili for a dinner, a party, a movie, or game night. A topping bar is fun, too!

Makes 8 cups

Onion 1 medium

Red bell pepper 1 medium

Garlic cloves 3 medium

Vegetable oil 2 tablespoons

Ground meat such as turkey, chicken, beef, or pork; 1 pound

Chili powder 2½ tablespoons

Cumin ground, 1 teaspoon

Oregano dried, ½ teaspoon

Salt ½ teaspoon

Black beans 15-ounce can

Kidney beans 15-ounce can

Diced tomatoes and their juice 28-ounce can

Tomato paste 2 tablespoons

Water 1 cup

Toppings such as scallions, tomatoes, avocado, cheese, sour cream, salsa, or corn chips

 Ask an adult to help with the knives, grater, stove, and boiling chili.

1. **Prep the veggies and toppings.** Wash the vegetables. Peel the onion. Chop the onion and bell pepper. Peel and mince the garlic. Set them all aside. If using toppings, chop the veggies, grate the cheese, and put each one in a separate dish.

2. **Cook the meat.** Measure the oil into a large pot, set the burner to medium-high, and heat for 30 seconds. Add the meat and cook for 6 to 8 minutes (or until it's no longer pink), stirring and breaking up the meat. Turn the heat down to medium-low.

3. **Add the veggies and spices.** Stir in the onion, bell pepper, and garlic, and let the mixture cook for 10 minutes or until the veggies are very soft, stirring often. Stir in the seasonings, including salt. Cook 1 more minute.

4. **Add the canned foods and water.** Pour the beans into a colander, rinse with cold water, let them drain for a minute, and add them to the pot. Add the tomatoes and their juice. Add the tomato paste and the water. Stir well. Turn the heat up to medium-high. Once the chili boils, turn the burner to a very low setting. Partially cover the pot with a lid, set a timer for 45 minutes, and let it simmer. Stir the chili often so that it doesn't stick to the pot and burn.

5. **Serve with the toppings.** After the chili is thick, set out the toppings at the table. Ladle the chili into bowls, and invite guests to choose their own toppings.

Italian minestrone

No soup accommodates the seasons better than minestrone. You can add or leave out vegetables depending on what's in season, what's in the fridge, or what vegetables you like to eat.

Makes 8 cups

Onion 1 medium

Garlic 2 cloves

Carrots 2 medium

Celery 1 stalk

Green vegetables such as beans or zucchini, 2 cups total

Extra-virgin olive oil 2 tablespoons, plus extra to drizzle

Thyme dried, 1 teaspoon

Oregano dried, 1 teaspoon

Basil dried, ½ teaspoon

Tomato sauce 8-ounce can

Diced tomatoes and their juice 15-ounce can

Chicken broth 4 cups

Beans such as kidney, navy, or cannelloni; 15-ounce can

Pasta small shape such as ditalini or small shells, uncooked, ½ cup

Salt 1 teaspoon

Ground black pepper ¼ teaspoon

Parmesan cheese grated or shredded for garnish, ¼ cup

Ask an adult to help with the knives, grater, hot liquid, and stove.

1. **Prep the veggies.** Wash all the veggies. Peel the onion, garlic, and carrots. Mince the garlic, and chop the other veggies into bite-size pieces. Rinse the beans in a colander with cold water, and drain.

2. **Start cooking.** Pour oil into a large pot, set the heat to medium-low, and add the onion, garlic, carrots, celery, and herbs. Cook for 10 minutes, or until the onion is soft, stirring often.

3. **Add ingredients.** Add the tomato sauce, diced tomatoes with their juice, chicken broth, drained beans, and green vegetables. Turn the heat up to high. As soon as the soup boils, turn the heat to low and simmer for 5 minutes.

4. **Cook the pasta.** Turn the heat to high again. When the soup boils, carefully add the pasta—don't splash yourself! Stir so that the pasta doesn't stick to the bottom of the pot. Turn the heat to medium-low, cover, and let the soup cook. After 8 minutes, test a noodle. If it's firm and tender, the soup is done.

5. **Add the finishing touches.** Stir in the salt and pepper. Ladle soup into bowls, and top each with a drizzle of olive oil and a sprinkle of Parmesan for extra flavor.

quick chick soup

Hot chicken-noodle soup tastes great with a sandwich for lunch. But if someone in your family is under the weather, make this!

Chicken or vegetable broth 2 cups

Egg noodles uncooked, 1 cup

Parsley fresh, ½ teaspoon

 Ask an adult to help with the stove and boiling soup.

1. **Prep the parsley.** Wash the parsley, and tear a few leaves into tiny bits. Set aside.

2. **Boil the broth.** Pour the broth into a medium saucepan, and bring it to a boil over high heat.

3. **Add the noodles.** Stir in the noodles. (Don't splash yourself!) Turn the heat to low, add the parsley, and let the soup simmer for 5 to 10 minutes, or until the noodles are tender.

4. **Serve.** Ladle the soup into a bowl. Careful—this soup will be hot!

meats & mains

mac & cheese
32

pizza! pizza! pizza!
34

taco fest
36

coconut curry shrimp
38

spaghetti marinara
40

three-cheese lasagna
42

lemon-roasted chicken
44

crunchy chicken salad
46

mac & cheese

Is there a yummier comfort food than macaroni and cheese? Make a green vegetable or green salad while the casserole bakes, and be warned: Your family might ask for this meal every week!

Makes 4 to 6 servings

Elbow macaroni uncooked, 2 cups

Salt 2 teaspoons for the macaroni cooking water, plus ½ teaspoon for the mac & cheese

Milk 1 cup

Heavy cream 1 cup

Cheddar cheese grated, 3 cups

Mix-in ingredients such as ham, chicken, or cooked onions, peas, or broccoli; 1 cup total

All-purpose flour 2 tablespoons

Vegetable-oil spray

Panko bread crumbs ½ cup

 Ask an adult to help with the grater, stove, boiling water, and oven.

1. **Turn on the oven.** Preheat to 350 degrees.

2. **Cook the pasta.** Fill a large pot three-fourths full with cold water, place it on the stove, and add 2 teaspoons of salt. Cover the pot, and bring the water to a rolling boil over high heat. Carefully add the pasta—don't splash yourself! Stir so that the pasta doesn't stick to the bottom of the pot. When the water boils again, turn the heat down to medium-high. After 8 minutes, test a noodle. If it's firm and tender, empty the macaroni into a colander that's placed in the sink. Rinse briefly with cool water, let it drain, and pour it into a large mixing bowl.

3. **Combine the ingredients.** Stir the milk, heavy cream, ½ teaspoon salt, cheese, and any mix-in ingredients into the bowl with the macaroni. Sprinkle the flour over the mixture and stir until the ingredients are well blended.

4. **Prep the baking dish.** Lightly spray an 8-inch-by-8-inch baking dish with vegetable-oil spray for easier cleanup. Pour the macaroni and cheese mixture into the dish. Set aside.

5. **Prep the crumbs.** Heat a skillet on the stove on low. Add the crumbs and cook until they are brown and crispy, about 3 or 4 minutes. Spoon the crumbs over the top of the mac & cheese in the baking dish.

6. **Bake the casserole.** Put the casserole in the oven, and bake for 30 minutes. After the timer goes off, the edges of the casserole should be bubbling, and the center should feel firm when pressed with the back of a spoon. Serve it hot at the table!

THIS MAC & CHEESE IS MADE WITH HAM & PEAS!

THIS PIZZA IS MADE WITH PEPPERONI AND GREEN BELL PEPPER!

pizza! pizza! pizza!

It's easy to order a delivery pizza or bake a frozen one, but making pizza is so much fun—and easy! Divide the dough ball for personal pizzas, or divide a large pizza into sections with different toppings.

Pizza dough 1-pound ball

All-purpose flour ¼ cup

Vegetable shortening for greasing the baking sheet

Pizza sauce store-bought or marinara on page 40, ½ cup

Mozzarella cheese grated, 1 cup

Parmesan cheese grated, ¼ cup

Toppings optional, such as ham, pepperoni, mushrooms, olives, onion, green bell pepper, fresh basil leaves, and tomato slices

 Ask an adult to help with the knives, grater, stove, and oven.

1. **Get things to the right temperature.** If your dough is refrigerated, let it sit at room temperature for 20 minutes before you handle it. Place a rack in the middle of the oven, and preheat the oven to 425 degrees.

2. **Stretch the dough.** With the shortening, lightly grease a large baking sheet, with or without sides. Place the flour in a bowl and dust your hands with it. Pick up the dough ball and lightly dust it with the flour, too. Place the dough in the middle of the baking sheet. Push, pull, and stretch it so that it fills the sheet. Don't worry if the pizza isn't in an even shape—that's part of the fun.

3. **Add the toppings.** Spoon on the sauce, and gently spread it around so that it's near the edge of the dough but not touching. Add any optional toppings. Last, sprinkle the cheeses evenly over the sauce and toppings.

4. **Bake the pizza.** Bake for 18 to 20 minutes, or until the cheese in the middle of the pizza is bubbly with brown spots and the crust edges are golden brown. Slide the baked pizza onto a cutting board, and cut into wedges to serve.

taco fest

Each time you fix tacos for family or friends, try different fillings. Use leftover fish or chicken. Add coleslaw or jicama and apple. Use corn or flour tortillas. Try a mango or green salsa. Keep diners guessing!

Makes 8 tacos

Onion 1 small

Tomato 1 large

Cilantro fresh, ¼ cup

Lettuce ½ small head

Avocado 1 medium

Limes 2 medium

Cheese such as cheddar, Jack, or feta; 1 cup

Sour cream ½ cup

Salsa 1 cup

Tortillas soft corn, hard shells, or both; 8 total

Canned beans such as black, pinto, or refried; 1 cup

Cooked meat such as chopped or ground chicken, beef, or turkey; 2 to 3 cups

Taco seasoning 1 packet

Vegetable oil 1 tablespoon

 Ask an adult to help with the knives, grater, stove, oven, and pre-cooking.

1. **Prep the toppings.** Wash the veggies. Peel and chop the onion. Chop the tomato, cilantro, and lettuce. Dice the avocado. Cut each lime into 8 wedges. Grate the cheese. As you prepare each topping, place it in a separate serving bowl. Put the sour cream and salsa into bowls, too. Arrange the bowls on the dining table.

2. **Heat the tortillas.** *For soft tortillas:* Turn on the oven to 200 degrees. Wrap the tortillas in aluminum foil, and put them in the oven until you are ready to use them—or 5 to 7 minutes. *For hard tortillas:* Follow the directions on the taco-shell package.

3. **Heat the beans.** Drain the beans, and heat them in a small pan over low heat. Cook 4 minutes or until they're hot. Pour the beans into a bowl, and add them to the taco bar.

4. **Warm the cooked meat.** Put the pre-cooked meat and the taco seasoning into a mixing bowl, and stir until evenly coated. Put the oil in a skillet and set it over medium heat. After 30 seconds, add the meat. Stir for 3 to 4 minutes or until the meat is hot. Spoon the meat into a bowl, and place it on the taco bar.

5. **Finish the tortillas and serve.** Remove the tortillas from the oven. Use oven mitts to remove the foil from the soft tortillas, and then rewrap them in a clean cloth napkin or dish towel. Put hard tortillas on a plate. Now you're ready for a fiesta!

coconut curry shrimp

This dish looks like it came from your favorite Thai restaurant!

Rice uncooked, 1 cup

Unsweetened coconut shredded, 2 tablespoons

Cilantro 2 tablespoons

Scallions 3 medium

Ginger 1-inch piece

Garlic cloves 4 medium

Broccoli 2 cups

Sugar snap peas 2½ cups

Vegetable oil 1 tablespoon

Shrimp uncooked, medium size, peeled and de-veined, fresh or thawed from frozen; 1 pound

Curry powder 1 tablespoon

Salt ½ teaspoon

Ground black pepper ¼ teaspoon

Coconut milk 13.5-ounce can

Chicken or vegetable broth ½ cup

 Ask an adult to help with the knives, stove, and boiling liquid.

1. **Cook the rice.** Follow the directions on the package. When the rice is done, turn off the burner and move the pan to the back of the stove to stay warm.

2. **Toast the coconut.** Heat the oven to 350 degrees. Spread the coconut on a baking sheet, set the timer for 8 minutes, and slide the sheet into the oven. Stir the coconut a couple of times. Remove when the timer sounds, or when the coconut is light golden brown. Put it in a bowl and set aside.

3. **Prep the veggies.** Wash and chop the cilantro and scallions, put them in their own little bowls, and set aside. Peel and mince the ginger and garlic, wash and chop the broccoli, and wash the peas and cut them in half. Put the ginger, garlic, broccoli, and peas together in one bowl and set aside.

4. **Cook!** Set a large skillet over medium-high heat, and add the oil. After 30 seconds, add the shrimp, ginger, garlic, broccoli, and peas. Cook 4 to 5 minutes, or until the shrimp has just turned from clear to white and pink, stirring gently the entire time. Mix in the curry powder, salt, and pepper, and cook 30 seconds more.

5. **Add the liquids.** Pour in the coconut milk and broth, turn the heat up to high, and bring the curry to a boil. Once it boils, reduce the heat to low, and simmer for 3 to 4 minutes. The broccoli should be tender but still crunchy.

6. **Put it all together.** Divide the rice among four bowls, and top with the hot curry mixture. Sprinkle with toasted coconut, cilantro, and scallions, and serve right away.

39

spaghetti marinara

Homemade marinara sauce tastes much better than anything in a jar.
Freeze it to use for pizza, meatballs, lasagna, and more spaghetti!

Makes enough for 1 pound of spaghetti or about 6 to 8 servings

Onion 1 medium

Garlic cloves 3 medium

Carrot 1 medium

Diced tomatoes and their juice
28-ounce can

Extra-virgin olive oil
3 tablespoons

Basil dried, ¼ teaspoon

Oregano dried, ½ teaspoon

Spaghetti uncooked, 1 pound

Salt for the spaghetti cooking
water, 2 teaspoons

Parmesan cheese grated, about
½ cup

 Ask an adult to help with the knives, peeler, grater,
boiling water, and stove.

1. **Prep the veggies.** Peel and dice the onion. Peel and mince the
   garlic. Wash and grate the carrot. Use a potato masher to break
   the tomatoes into small pieces in a bowl.

2. **Cook the veggies.** Add the oil, onion, garlic, and carrot to a large
   saucepan, and stir to coat. Cook over medium heat for 5 minutes,
   stirring often. Add the tomatoes, basil, and oregano to the pot.

3. **Simmer the sauce.** Turn the heat up to high, and cook the sauce until it's bubbling around the edges. Then reduce the heat to low. Partially cover the pot with a lid, and let the sauce simmer for 30 to 45 minutes. Stir the sauce periodically to make sure it doesn't stick to the bottom of the pan and burn.

4. **Cook the spaghetti.** While the sauce is simmering, fill a large pot ¾ full with cold water. Add the salt, and heat on high until the water comes to a rolling boil. Carefully add the pasta—don't splash yourself! As soon as the pasta softens, use a long-handled spoon to push it under the water. When the water boils again, lower the heat slightly to medium-high. After 8 minutes, test a noodle. If it's firm and tender, empty the pasta into a colander that's placed in the sink.

5. **Put it together.** Put grated Parmesan in a small serving bowl with a spoon for the table. Fill one large bowl or individual pasta bowls with spaghetti. Ladle the sauce over the pasta, and serve.

three-cheese lasagna

Make this lasagna for a family dinner or a girls' night supper.
Serve with crusty garlic bread and a salad.

Makes 8 servings

Lasagna noodles 12 no-boil sheets

Parmesan cheese grated, 1 cup

Mozzarella cheese grated, 1 cup

Marinara sauce 28-ounce can or recipe on page 40, 3½ cups

Ricotta cheese whole milk or part skim, 15-ounce container

Ask an adult to help with the grater and oven.

1. Turn on the oven. Place a rack in the middle of the oven. Preheat to 375 degrees.

2. Layer the lasagna. Build the lasagna in a 9-inch-by-13-inch baking dish, following these 12 steps. Start at the bottom!

12. Sprinkle all of the grated mozzarella across the top.

11. Add the last of the sauce, about 1 cup.

10. Top with the last 4 lasagna sheets.

9. Sprinkle on the remaining Parmesan.

8. Add a second layer of ricotta, using it up.

7. Spread on 1 cup of sauce.

6. Cover with 4 more overlapping lasagna sheets.

5. Sprinkle on ½ cup grated Parmesan.

4. Spoon on 1 cup of ricotta in small blobs.

3. Spread on ¾ cup of sauce.

2. Lay 4 lasagna sheets in the dish. Overlap the edges slightly.

1. Spread ¾ cup of sauce in the baking dish.

3. Heat and serve. Cover the dish with foil, and put it into the oven. Set the timer for 30 minutes. After the timer goes off, remove the foil, bake the lasagna for 10 minutes more, and then remove it from the oven. Let the lasagna cool for 5 minutes. Then cut it into 8 pieces. Serve from the dish with a wide spatula.

lemon-roasted chicken

While this chicken roasts, you'll have time to make side dishes. In the summer, serve with tomato slices and rice pilaf. In colder months, make mashed potatoes and a cooked vegetable.

Whole chicken 3½ to 4 pounds

Lemon 1 medium

Garlic 6 medium cloves

Fresh thyme loose handful of sprigs

Butter softened, 2 tablespoons

Salt ½ teaspoon

Ground black pepper ¼ teaspoon

Kitchen string about 12 inches

 Ask an adult to help with knives, scissors, the oven, a meat thermometer, and handling raw chicken.

1. **Prep the ingredients.** Wash the lemon and cut it in half crosswise. Peel the garlic cloves, but don't cut them. Wash the thyme and set aside a few sprigs for garnish. Measure the butter and place it in its own dish. Measure the salt and pepper and combine them into another small dish. Place all of these ingredients next to the sink.

2. **Set up the chicken.*** Preheat the oven to 425 degrees. If you use a roasting rack (it's optional), put it inside the roasting pan. Cut a piece of kitchen string about 12 inches long. Set the pan and string next to the sink, near all of your ingredients from step 1. Unwrap the chicken in a clean sink, pull the packet of giblets out of the cavity, and throw it away. Place the chicken in the pan.

3. **Stuff the chicken.** Put the lemon halves, garlic cloves, and thyme (all except the garnish sprigs) inside the chicken.

4. **Butter the chicken.** Turn the chicken to one side, rub on the butter, and sprinkle with salt and pepper. Then turn the chicken to the other side and do the same. Place the chicken breast-side up, and butter the breast. Last, use the string to tie the drumsticks together. **Now wash up!***

* When working with raw chicken, wash your hands often, very thoroughly, and with warm water and soap. Do the same with tools and work surfaces. Have all of your ingredients measured and nearby, and your tools at hand, before you touch the chicken.

5. Roast the chicken. Put the pan into the oven. Set a timer for 55 minutes. When the timer sounds and if the chicken looks brown and juicy, insert a meat thermometer deep into the thigh but without touching the bone. If it reads less than 165 degrees, return the chicken to the oven and check again in 5 to 10 minutes. Once it does read 165, take the chicken out of the oven, place a tent of foil over it, and let it sit for 10 minutes. Garnish with thyme and serve.

crunchy chicken salad

Use leftover Lemon-Roasted Chicken for this Asian-style dish that's a complete meal in one bowl. Get creative by adding salad items such as sliced radishes, celery, and snow peas.

Makes 4 to 6 servings

Chicken cooked, 2 cups

Bell pepper 1 small

Carrots shredded, 1½ cups

Cole slaw veggie mix 2 cups

Edamame shelled, ¾ cup

Cashew pieces ⅓ cup

Asian Vinaigrette (recipe on page 56)

Crispy rice or chow mein noodles 1 cup

 Ask an adult to help with slicing and chopping.

1. **Prep the ingredients.** Wash and slice the bell pepper. Chop the cooked chicken. Make the vinaigrette.

2. **Mix it up.** In a large bowl, toss together all the ingredients except the vinaigrette and crispy noodles.

3. **Add the finishing touches.** Drizzle the vinaigrette over the salad, and toss well. Sprinkle with the crispy noodles and serve.

salads & sides

nutty rice pilaf
48

gorgeous greens
50

ridiculously rich mashed potatoes
52

seasonal salads
54

better-than-bottled vinaigrettes
56

green goddess & veggies
58

nutty rice pilaf

Rice becomes pilaf when you cook it in broth and butter or oil, and add onions, spices, and nuts for a rich flavor.

Makes 4 servings

Onion 1 small

Carrots 2 medium

Parsley or scallions or a mix, 2 tablespoons total

Nuts such as almonds, walnuts, or pecans; 6 tablespoons

Salted butter 2 tablespoons

Rice uncooked, 1 cup

Chicken or vegetable broth 2 cups

Salt ¼ teaspoon

 Ask an adult to help with knives, the stove, and boiling liquid.

1. **Prep the veggies.** Wash the veggies. Peel and dice the onion and the carrots. Chop the parsley or scallions.

2. **Prep the nuts.** Place a large skillet on the stove, and heat on medium-high. When the skillet is hot, add the nuts in a single layer. Toast them 1 to 2 minutes, stirring often, until they are golden brown and smelling nutty. Remove them from the pan and let them cool. Chop them into small pieces.

3. **Sauté the veggies and rice.** Melt the butter in a saucepan over medium-low heat. Add the onion and carrots. Cook 5 minutes or until the onion seems almost clear, stirring often. Stir in the uncooked rice, reduce the heat to low, and cook for 2 minutes.

4. **Cook.** Stir in the broth and salt, turn the burner up to high, and let the mixture come to a boil. Then reduce the heat all the way to low, cover the pan tightly, and set the timer for 15 minutes.

5. **Stir in the additions.** After the timer sounds, turn off the heat and let the rice rest for 3 minutes. Then sprinkle in the parsley, scallions, and nuts, stirring and fluffing the rice at the same time. Spoon the pilaf into a pretty bowl and serve.

gorgeous greens

A vegetable seasoned with salt and pepper is delicious. But mix in herbs, nuts, or fruits, and suddenly you're thinking like a chef!

Makes 6 to 8 servings

Green vegetable such as green beans, asparagus, broccoli, snow peas, or sugar snap peas; 1 pound

Salt ½ teaspoon

Butter or extra-virgin olive oil 1 to 2 tablespoons

Ground black pepper pinch

ADD-INS!

#1: SLICED ALMONDS, 2 tablespoons
TOP WITH: LEMON ZEST, 1 or 2 teaspoons

#2: FRESH GINGER, minced, 1 tablespoon
SOY SAUCE, 1 tablespoon
TOP WITH: SCALLION, sliced, 1 medium

#3: FRESH GARLIC, minced, 1 tablespoon
TOP WITH: FRESH THYME, 1 or 2 teaspoons

Ask an adult to help with the knives, boiling water, and stove.

1. **Prep the greens.** Wash the greens. Cut off tough or dry ends, remove any brown leaves, or pull off tough strings. Cut broccoli into florets, or snap off the tough ends of asparagus stems.

2. **Cook the greens.** Fill a pan half full with water. Add the salt. Bring the water to a rolling boil on high heat. Carefully add the veggies. (Don't splash yourself!) Turn the heat to medium and cook for 3 to 5 minutes, only until the greens are tender and bright—but no longer. When the veggies are ready, drain them in a colander in the sink.

3. **Give the veggies an ice bath.** To stop the greens from cooking, fill a mixing bowl halfway with ice and water, and put the veggies into the bowl. Let them chill completely and then drain well.

4. **Cook add-ins.** In a skillet on medium, heat 1 tablespoon of butter or oil—more, if needed to cover the bottom of the pan well. If using garlic or ginger, add it now, and cook for 30 seconds. Add the greens, and stir for 4 minutes. Stir in any other add-in ingredients, and then remove the skillet from the heat. Season with pepper, place veggies in a serving dish, and finish with a tasty topping.

THIS DISH IS MADE WITH GREEN BEANS, SLICED ALMONDS, AND LEMON ZEST!

ridiculously rich mashed potatoes

Pair these dreamy potatoes with a main dish, or serve bowls of the potatoes with grated cheddar cheese, diced chicken, sour cream, crumbled bacon, or steamed broccoli.

Makes 6 to 8 servings

Yukon Gold potatoes 3 pounds (about 8 medium)

Salt 1 teaspoon for the boiling water, plus ½ teaspoon for seasoning

Half & half 1 cup

Butter 2 tablespoons (¼ stick), plus a small pat for garnish

Ground black pepper ¼ teaspoon

Parsley fresh, chopped, ½ teaspoon

 Ask an adult to help with the knives, stove, and boiling water.

1. **Prep the potatoes.** Wash, peel, and cut the potatoes into big chunks, and place them in a large pot. Add cold water until the potatoes are just covered. Add 1 teaspoon of salt and stir.

2. **Boil the potatoes.** Put a lid on the pot, and bring the water to boil over high heat. Once it boils, turn the heat to low. Let the potatoes cook about 12 minutes or until they're tender. (To test, stick a small knife into the middle of a large chunk.) When done, pour the potatoes into a colander in the sink, and leave them to drain and steam. Do not rinse!

3. **Heat the dairy.** Put the half & half and butter in a saucepan, and turn the heat to medium. After the butter melts and the mixture is steaming heavily, turn off the heat. Make sure it doesn't boil.

4. **Mash the potatoes.** When the potatoes have stopped steaming and they look dry, return them to their cooking pot. Mash them for a minute with a potato masher, and then pour in about half of the hot dairy mixture. Mash some more, and add more dairy. Continue until the potatoes are smooth and the dairy is gone. Add the salt and pepper for seasoning, and stir thoroughly.

5. **Garnish.** Spoon the potatoes into a serving bowl and garnish with a small pat of butter and a sprinkling of chopped fresh parsley.

seasonal salads

Seasonal ingredients and seasoned vinaigrettes
make these salads special all year round!

 Ask an adult to help with the knives, stove, and boiling water.

Winter Salad

Salad greens 6 cups

Granny Smith apple chopped,
1 medium

Dried cranberries 3 tablespoons

Pecans toasted (directions
on page 56, "Toasted Sesame
Seeds") and chopped, ⅓ cup

French Vinaigrette (recipe
on page 57; use cider vinegar
instead of red-wine vinegar)

Spring Salad

Salad greens 6 cups

Scallions sliced thin,
3 medium

Asparagus boiled 1 minute
and chopped, 12 spears

Hard-boiled egg chopped, 1
(directions on page 23)

Clementine 1, in sections

Asian or Orange Vinaigrette
(recipes on pages 56–57)

Summer Salad

Salad greens 6 cups

Feta cheese crumbled, ½ cup

Cucumber peeled and sliced, ¾ cup

Watermelon chunks 1½ cups

French Vinaigrette (recipe on page 57; use fresh lemon juice instead of red-wine vinegar)

Fall Salad

Salad greens 6 cups

Corn kernels fresh, ½ cup

Cherry tomatoes chopped, 6 to 8

Pita chips broken pieces, 1 cup

French Vinaigrette (recipe on page 57)

1. **Prep the greens.** Wash the leaves, and dry them in a salad spinner or with a clean dish towel. Move them to a bowl. Tear any big leaves into smaller pieces.

2. **Add mix-ins.** Choose a salad, and add the listed ingredients to the bowl. Just before serving, add the vinaigrette and toss.

better-than-bottled vinaigrettes

Making vinaigrette is kitchen magic. Take simple ingredients, whisk them together, and—*abracadabra!*—a delicious dressing.

 Ask an adult to help with the knives.

Asian Vinaigrette

Peanut oil 5 tablespoons

Toasted sesame oil 1 tablespoon

Rice-wine vinegar 3 tablespoons

Soy sauce 2 tablespoons

Garlic clove minced or crushed through a garlic press, 1 medium

Toasted sesame seeds 1 tablespoon

Scallion chopped, 1 tablespoon

Toasted Sesame Seeds

Set a skillet on the stove and turn heat to medium. Add the seeds to the pan in a single layer. Stir until they are golden brown—about 2 or 3 minutes. Remove from the pan. (Nuts can be toasted this way, too.)

French Vinaigrette

Olive oil 6 tablespoons

Red-wine vinegar 3 tablespoons

Garlic clove minced or crushed through a garlic press, 1 medium

Dijon mustard 1 teaspoon

Salt pinch

Ground black pepper pinch

Fresh herbs such as thyme, parsley, or basil, minced; 1 tablespoon

Orange Vinaigrette

Olive oil 6 tablespoons

Orange juice 3 tablespoons

Lemon juice 1 tablespoon

Honey 1 teaspoon

Dijon mustard 1 teaspoon

Salt pinch

Ground black pepper pinch

Shallot minced, 1 tablespoon

1. **Blend the dressing.** Put all the ingredients into a bowl with high sides and whisk well, or put them into a jar, tighten the lid, and shake well.

2. **Toss and serve.** Just before serving, whisk or shake the dressing again, and pour it onto the salad a little at a time. Toss the salad after each addition of dressing. Stop adding dressing when the lettuce leaves are just lightly coated.

green goddess & veggies

This condiment is yummy as a dip, a dressing, and a sauce!

Makes about 1½ cups

Cut vegetables for dipping such as carrots, celery, sugar snap peas, cucumber, and bell peppers

Dill fresh, loosely packed, ¼ cup

Parsley fresh, loosely packed, ½ cup

Garlic cloves 2 medium

Mayonnaise 1 cup

Plain Greek yogurt ½ cup

White vinegar 1 tablespoon

Salt ¼ teaspoon

Ground black pepper pinch

 Ask an adult to help with knives and the blender.

1. **Prep the veggies.** Wash and trim any vegetables you want to serve with the dip. Cut the veggies into sizes and shapes that are best for dipping.

2. **Blend and serve.** Wash the herbs and peel the garlic cloves. Add them with the remaining ingredients to a blender container, put on the top, and whirl on high until the dip is smooth. Pour the dip into a bowl, and serve with the veggies.

sips & snacks

lip-smacking lemonades
60

garlicky white bean dip
62

fresh guacamole
64

quick quesadilla
66

crispy cheese toast
68

Simple syrup makes crafting these summer sippers a cinch.

hot-day lemonade

Makes about 2 quarts or 8 cups

Sugar 1 cup

Boiling water 1 cup

Lemons 5 to 8, enough for 1¼ cups of juice

Cold water 6 cups

Lemon slices or mint sprigs (optional for garnish)

 Ask an adult to help with the boiling water.

1. **Make a simple syrup.** Put the sugar into a tempered glass or ceramic container, and add the boiling water. Stir well. Set aside to dissolve.

2. **Squeeze the lemons.** Set a sieve over a stable bowl. Roll the lemons on a flat surface, pressing with your palm, to break up the fibers for easier juicing. Cut the lemons in half crosswise, and use a reamer to squeeze the juice over the sieve and into the bowl.

3. **Stir and serve.** Add the syrup, lemon juice, and cold water to a 12-cup or larger pitcher. Stir well, and serve over ice. Garnish with lemon or mint, if desired.

strawberry lemonade

Makes about 1½ quarts or 6 cups

Fresh or frozen strawberries sliced, 2 cups, plus extras for garnish

Lemonade homemade or store-bought, 1 quart

 Ask an adult to help with the blender.

1. **Prep the berries.** Wash fresh berries, cut off the stems and any tough parts below the stems. Cut all the fruit in half.

2. **Blend.** Put the strawberries in a blender, add 1 cup of lemonade, and whirl on high until you have a smooth purée.

3. **Stir in the purée and serve.** Pour the strawberry purée into the remaining lemonade, and stir well. Serve in glasses over ice. For a garnish, make a cut in a strawberry and slip it over the edge of the glass.

garlicky white bean dip

Prepare a bowl of this dip for parties, game night, or a delicious snack. Serve it with crackers, chips, or fresh-cut veggies.

Makes about 1½ cups

Dippers veggies, toasted bread, crackers, or pita chips

Garlic cloves 2 medium

Scallion 1 medium

Cannellini beans 15-ounce can

Lemons 1 or 2, enough for 2 tablespoons of juice

Olive oil 2 tablespoons

Salt ¼ teaspoon

Ground black pepper pinch

 Ask an adult to help with the blender.

1. **Prep the dippers.** Wash, trim, and chop any veggies you want as dippers. Toast and cut bread or pita dippers into triangles, if desired. Set all dippers aside.

2. **Squeeze the lemons.** Set a sieve over a stable bowl. Roll the lemons on a flat surface, pressing with your palm, to break up the fibers for easier juicing. Cut the lemons in half crosswise, and use a reamer to squeeze the juice over the sieve and into the bowl.

3. **Combine the dip ingredients.** Peel the garlic. Trim and slice the scallion. Pour the beans into a sieve or colander; rinse with cold water and let drain well. Put the beans into a blender, and add the lemon juice, garlic, scallion, oil, salt, and pepper.

4. **Process and serve.** Run the blender on high for 20 seconds. Stop it, remove the lid, and use a rubber spatula to scrape down the sides. Replace the lid securely and blend until very smooth. Spoon the dip into a bowl, and serve on a platter with dippers around it.

fresh guacamole

Guacamole is delicious all day! You can smear it on a bagel with cheese for breakfast, on toast with turkey for lunch, on quesadillas or tacos for dinner, and with chips or veggies for a yummy snack.

Makes about 1½ cups

Hass avocados ripe, 2 medium

Scallions 2 medium

Tomato 1 small

Cilantro fresh, 1 tablespoon

Limes 1 or 2, enough for 2 tablespoons of juice

Salt ¼ teaspoon

Hot sauce (optional)

 Ask an adult to help with knives.

1. **Prep the veggies.** Run the paring knife around the avocado, twist it open, remove the large seed (called the pit), scoop out the flesh, and put it into a medium-size bowl. Wash, trim, and finely chop the scallions, tomato, and cilantro. Set aside.

2. **Squeeze the limes.** Set a sieve over a stable bowl. Roll the limes on a flat surface, pressing with your palm, to break up the fibers for easier juicing. Cut the limes in half crosswise, and use a reamer to squeeze the juice over the sieve and into the bowl.

3. **Combine the ingredients.** Mash up the avocados with a fork. It's fine if the mash is lumpy. Stir in the scallions, tomato, cilantro, lime juice, and salt. Add a dash of hot sauce, if desired.

TIP!
Guacamole quickly turns brown, so if you're not serving it right away, cover the dip bowl with plastic wrap, seal the edges, and refrigerate. Just before serving, scrape off any dark areas. They would taste fine but may look less appetizing.

quick quesadilla

With only a few ingredients, you can make a gooey, crunchy, and totally delicious snack or meal that'll satisfy even the pickiest eater.

Makes one 8-inch quesadilla

Cheddar cheese grated, ½ cup

Black beans canned, ¼ cup

Veggies such as tomatoes, corn kernels, scallions, and spinach; ½ cup total

Vegetable-oil spray

Flour tortillas 2 medium (8-inch)

Condiments such as salsa, sour cream, guacamole, and hot sauce (optional)

 Ask an adult to help with knives and the stove.

1. **Prep the ingredients.** Pour the beans into a sieve or colander in the sink, rinse with cold water, and let them drain well. Wash the veggies; finely chop them, if needed.

2. **Fill the tortilla.** Lightly coat a skillet or griddle with vegetable-oil spray. Lay one tortilla in the pan. Sprinkle on the grated cheese, beans, and veggies. Cover with the second tortilla.

3. **Heat the quesadilla.** Turn on a burner to medium heat, and cook the quesadilla for 3 to 5 minutes or until the cheese has melted and the bottom has toasty brown spots. Then carefully but quickly flip the quesadilla with a spatula. If anything falls out, just tuck it back in later. Cook the second side for 2 minutes or until toasty brown.

4. **Cut and serve.** Move the quesadilla to a cutting board to cool a few minutes. Then cut it into wedges and serve with condiments.

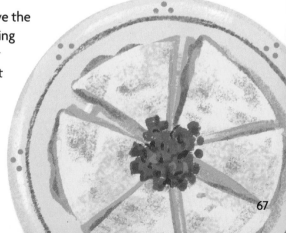

crispy cheese toast

This snack or side tastes too good to be so easy to make.

Makes 2 slices

Butter softened, 2 teaspoons

Cheese cook's choice, grated, ½ cup

Mayonnaise 1 tablespoon

Bread 2 slices

 Ask an adult to help with the oven.

1. **Turn on the oven.** Preheat an oven or toaster oven to 400 degrees.

2. **Prep the bread.** Put the butter, cheese, and mayo into a bowl, and stir to blend well. Spread half the cheese onto each slice of bread.

3. **Toast the bread.** Cover a baking sheet with foil, lay the bread on it, and bake 5 minutes or until the cheese is bubbly and brown. Remove the pan from the oven, move the bread onto plates with a spatula, and serve. Watch out—the cheese will be hot!

sweets & treats

oatmeal chocolate chippers
70

apple-blueberry crisp
72

peachy parfait
74

chocolate-chocolate cupcakes
76

chocolate velvet frosting
78

oatmeal chocolate chippers

This recipe makes a lot of cookies, but they'll go fast!

Makes 60 cookies

Unsalted butter softened to room temperature, 1¼ cups (2½ sticks)

Granulated sugar 1½ cups

Brown sugar packed, 1 cup

All-purpose flour 2 cups

Baking powder 1 teaspoon

Baking soda ½ teaspoon

Salt ½ teaspoon

Eggs 2 large

Pure vanilla extract 2 teaspoons

Old-fashioned rolled oats (not quick-cooking or instant) 3 cups

Chocolate chips 2 cups or a 10-ounce bag

Vegetable-oil spray

 Ask an adult to help with the mixer and oven.

1. **Get the oven ready.** Position the oven rack in the center of the oven. Preheat it to 350 degrees.

2. **Beat the butter and sugars.** Put the butter and sugars into a deep bowl. Use a mixer to blend, starting on medium-low and then increasing to medium-high. Mix until the butter and sugars look smooth and creamy, about 4 minutes. Turn off the mixer a few times, and scrape the sides of the bowl with a rubber spatula.

3. **Whisk the dry ingredients.** In a separate medium-size mixing bowl, whisk together the flour, baking powder, baking soda, and salt until they are well blended.

4. **Combine all of the ingredients.** Add the eggs and vanilla to the butter and sugar mixture. Blend on medium-low for 2 minutes. Add a heaping spoonful of the dry ingredients to the wet mixture, and blend. Continue to add the dry ingredients in large spoonfuls, blending in before adding more, until all of the dry ingredients have been added. Scrape the sides of the bowl as needed. Last, stir in the uncooked oats and chocolate chips with a large spoon.

5. **Bake the cookies.** Lightly coat a baking sheet with vegetable-oil spray. Using a small spoon, drop equal-size spoonfuls of dough 2 inches apart on the sheet. Slide the sheet into the oven and set the timer for 16 minutes. When the cookies are done, the edges should be browned nicely.

6. **Cool.** When the cookies are done, place the sheet on the stove top to cool for 3 minutes. Then transfer the cookies to a cooling rack or a clean sheet of wax paper laid out on a flat surface. Use a second baking sheet for the next batch of cookies. Repeat until all of the dough is baked, alternating baking sheets between batches.

apple-blueberry crisp

Crisps and cobblers are like pies, only much easier. You can change the blueberries to blackberries or raspberries, and the apples to pears.

Makes 6 to 8 servings

Old-fashioned rolled oats (not quick-cooking or instant) ½ cup

Brown sugar packed, ½ cup

All-purpose flour ¼ cup, plus 1 tablespoon for the apples

Salt ¼ teaspoon

Unsalted butter cold, 4 tablespoons (½ stick)

Granny Smith apples 5 to 8, enough for 6 cups when sliced

Blueberries 2 cups

Granulated sugar ¼ cup

Cinnamon ground, 1 teaspoon

Vegetable-oil spray

Vanilla ice cream (optional)

 Ask an adult to help with the knives, peeler, and oven.

1. **Turn on the oven.** Preheat the oven to 350 degrees.

2. **Make the topping.** Put the uncooked oats, brown sugar, ¼ cup flour, and salt into a medium-size mixing bowl and stir. Cut very cold butter into small pieces, and add it to the oatmeal mixture. With clean fingers, rub the oatmeal mixture and butter together, pressing hard enough to mash the butter into small pieces but not enough to melt it or blend it in. Set aside.

3. **Prep the apples.** Peel the apples, cut them into quarters, and use a paring knife to cut out the core from each piece. Thinly slice the apples and place them in a separate, large mixing bowl.

4. **Mix and bake.** Add the blueberries, sugar, 1 tablespoon of flour, and cinnamon to the apples, and stir. Lightly coat an 8-inch-by-8-inch baking dish with vegetable-oil spray, and spoon in the fruit. Sprinkle the topping over the fruit, set the timer for 55 minutes, and bake. Perfect crisp has a browned top and bubbling edges. Remove the crisp from the oven, let it cool, and serve with ice cream, if you like.

peachy parfait

A parfait takes a little more time than a scoop of ice cream, but it makes a splashy and festive presentation!

Makes 4 servings

Raspberries 2 cups

Sliced peaches fresh, or frozen and thawed; 2 cups

Granulated sugar 2 tablespoons

Nutmeg ground, ⅛ teaspoon

Vanilla ice cream 3 cups

Vanilla wafer-roll cookies 4 whole

 Ask an adult to help with the knives.

1. **Wash and cut the fruit.** Remove any squishy raspberries and pick out any leaves. Wash the raspberries and let them drain well. Cut the fresh or thawed-from-frozen peaches into small chunks.

2. **Mix the fruit with spices.** In a medium mixing bowl, gently stir together the raspberries, peaches, sugar, and nutmeg. Cover and refrigerate for 30 minutes.

3. **Arrange the parfaits.** Spoon some of the fruit mixture into the bottom of four parfait glasses. Top each with a large scoop of ice cream. Spoon the remaining fruit on top.

4. **Add a cookie.** Stick a cookie into each parfait. Serve right away.

chocolate-chocolate cupcakes

Vanilla cupcakes are good, but chocolate rules! These cupcakes take longer to make than boxed ones, but they're much more delicious.

Makes 24 cupcakes

Unsalted butter softened, 1 cup

Granulated sugar 1½ cups

Eggs 4 large

Vanilla extract 1 teaspoon

All-purpose flour 2 cups

Salt ½ teaspoon

Baking soda 2 teaspoons

Unsweetened cocoa powder 1 cup

Milk 1½ cups

 Ask an adult to help with the mixer and oven.

1. **Prep the oven and pans.** Set one oven rack in the lower third of the oven, and set the other in the upper third. Preheat the oven to 350 degrees. Add cupcake liners to two 12-muffin pans.

2. **Beat the butter and sugar.** Put the butter and sugar into a deep mixing bowl, and beat on medium-high until light and creamy, about 4 minutes. Turn off the mixer a few times to scrape the sides of the bowl with a rubber spatula.

3. **Add the eggs and vanilla.** Crack an egg into a small bowl, and then add it to the butter mixture. Beat on medium for 30 seconds. Repeat with each egg until the batter is smooth again. Beat in the vanilla.

4. **Mix the dry ingredients.** In a separate medium-size bowl, whisk together the flour, salt, baking soda, and cocoa until well blended.

5. **Mix the dry with the wet.** Spoon half the flour mixture into the butter mixture and blend on low. Pour in half the milk; then add the rest of the flour mixture. Blend on low until nearly mixed, and then add the rest of the milk. Blend on medium for 20 seconds. Turn off the mixer, scrape the sides of the bowl, and blend again on medium for 1 minute.

6. **Bake and frost.** Use a small cup to fill the cupcake liners ⅔ full with the batter. Bake for 10 minutes. Then switch the cupcake positions—change racks and turn the pans around. Bake for 10 minutes more. Let cool for 30 minutes. Ice the cupcakes with Chocolate Velvet Frosting (recipe on page 78).

chocolate velvet frosting

Master this icing and you'll be ready for a cupcake competition!

Frosts 24 cupcakes

Unsweetened cocoa powder
2 cups

Powdered sugar 3½ cups
(1½ cups plus 2 cups)

Heavy cream 1 cup

Salted butter softened, 1 cup

Vanilla extract 2 teaspoons

Sprinkles or other decorations
(optional)

 Ask an adult to help with the stove.

1. **Mix the cocoa and sugar.** Set a sieve over a mixing bowl, and spoon in the cocoa and 1½ cups powdered sugar. Shake the sieve until all the cocoa and sugar go through it and into the bowl. (You can also use a sifter for this.) Set aside.

2. **Heat cream for the cocoa.** Pour the cream into a saucepan, and heat on medium until bubbles form around the edges and steam rises off the surface. Then pour the cream into the cocoa mixture and whisk until it's smooth and thick. Set aside for 10 minutes so that the mixture can cool to room temperature.

3. **Beat the sugar and butter.** While the cocoa cream is cooling, put the butter and the remaining 2 cups of powdered sugar into a large mixing bowl, and beat on high until smooth and fluffy. Beat in the vanilla.

4. **Add the cocoa cream.** With the mixer running on low, carefully add the cocoa cream a spoonful at a time. Turn off the mixer, scrape the sides of the bowl with a spatula, and then beat at medium speed for 1 minute more. If your cupcakes are completely cooled, they are ready for frosting! If you like, add sprinkles or other decorations for extra fun.

Which was your favorite recipe? Tell us!

Want us to cook up even more recipes? Let us know!

Write to:
You're the Chef Editor
American Girl
8400 Fairway Place
Middleton, WI 53562

(All comments and suggestions received by American Girl may be used without compensation or acknowledgment. We're sorry, but photos can't be returned.)

Use this chart to convert the U.S. measurements in this book to their metric equivalents.

MEASUREMENTS

U.S.	Metric
¼ teaspoon	1.25 ml
½ teaspoon	2.5 ml
1 teaspoon	5 ml
1 tablespoon	15 ml
¼ cup	60 ml
½ cup	120 ml
1 cup	240 ml
1 quart	.95 l
1 gallon	3.8 l
1 inch	2.54 cm
1 ounce	28 g
1 pound	454 g

ml = milliliter
l = liter
cm = centimeter
g = gram

PAN SIZES

Inches	Centimeters
9 × 13	22 × 33
8 × 8	20 × 20

OVEN TEMPERATURES

Fahrenheit	Celsius	Gas Mark
275°	140°	1 (low)
300°	150°	2
325°	165°	3
350°	180°	4 (medium)
375°	190°	5
400°	200°	6
425°	220°	7 (hot)
450°	230°	9
475°	240°	10 (very hot)

play@
☆ American Girl™

Discover online games, quizzes, activities, and more at **americangirl.com**